W9-AXV-395

ABCs of HALLOWEEN

Story and Art by Patricia Reeder Eubank

ideals children's books.
Nashville, Tennessee

ISBN-13: 978-0-8249-5658-5

Published by Ideals Children's Books
An imprint of Ideals Publications
A Guideposts Company
Nashville, Tennessee
www.idealsbooks.com

Copyright © 2013 by Patricia Reeder Eubank

Color separations by Precision Color Graphics,
Franklin, Wisconsin

Printed and bound in China

Designed by Eve DeGrie

Leo_May13_1

The Library of Congress has cataloged the hardcover edition of
this book as follows:

Eubank, Patti Reeder.
   ABCs of Halloween / by Patricia Reeder Eubank.
      p. cm.
Summary: Two young witches explore the alphabet of Halloween
from "attic" to the "zzz" at the end of their long day.
               (alk. paper)
   [1. Halloween—fiction. 2. Alphabet. 3. Stories in rhyme.]   I.
Title.
   PZ8.3.E88Ab 2003
   [E]—dc21
                                      2003007020

When Halloween comes near,
Two black cats read and peer
At the ABCs of treats and fun
That make Halloween loved
by everyone.

A is for attics—spooky, dusty, and dark.

B is for bats, blinking black cats, and broomsticks of hickory bark.

C is for candy, cobwebs, cracked cauldrons, and cackling witch cronies who screech when they speak.

D is for deep, dismal dungeons, dangerous dragons, and dreadful old doors that open and creak.

E is for evening shadows and eerie echoes that tingle your spine.

F is for frightening faces, flickering firelight, and fading footsteps that leave not a trace.

G is for glowing ghosts, glimmering ghouls, gurgling gargoyles, and groaning, green goblins galore.

H is for hollow, haunted houses
and crooked, high hats that
haggled-haired witches once wore.

I is for icy, ivory moonlight illuminating imaginary critters.

J is for jeering jack-o'-lanterns
giving you jolting,
jelly-kneed jitters.

K is for kindling kettles and keen kitchen witches who cook up a storm.

L is for lurking lizards and lightning bolts that make you wish you were home, safe, snug, and warm.

M is for mysterious, moaning monsters that meander up the stairs.

N is for nighttime noises
that make you nervous and
frizzle your hair.

O is for oval-eyed owls in old, gnarly oaks secretly watching you.

P is for perfect, plump pumpkins
and puzzling pirate potions—
purple, pale pink, and blue.

Q is for quiet whispers and quivering voices questioning every sound.

R is for raucous ravens, rickety rockers, and ripe, red apples, bobbing and rolling around.

S is for spinning spiders and scary skeletons with secret spells unbound.

T is for tiny toad toes, tasty turnip tea, and twisted tombstones that topple over the ground.

U is for umpteen, unseen unicorns undulating far across centuries of time.

V is for vain vampires and
vicious, thorny vines that
stealthily slither and climb.

W is for wild, wacky witches wandering the weird, windy night.

Extra-Good Alphabet Soup in a Pumpkin

Help Mom make this yummy soup. Slice off top of 1 medium pumpkin; clean out inside of pumpkin and set aside. Have Mom sauté 4 cut-up chicken breasts in 3 tablespoons of butter until golden. Remove and sauté 3 sliced carrots, 2 sliced celery stalks, and ½ cup scallions. Add 1 can each of cream of chicken soup, cream of celery soup, and chicken alphabet soup. Stir in 1 can water, ⅓ cup sour cream, and ½ teaspoon nutmeg. Mix well and pour into hollow pumpkin. Top with pumpkin top. Place on baking sheet and bake in a 350°F oven for 90 minutes. Scrape pumpkin sides when serving. Makes 8 servings.

X is for noodle x's floating in soup tasting just right.

EXTERIOR PAINT

Y is for young trick-or-treaters yowling and prowling far from the light.

Z is for Zemula and Zerelda,
two zonked-out zany
witches, snoring deeply
and sweetly after a long
Halloween night.